Digest

Also by Gregory Pardlo

Pencil of Rays and Spiked Mace, Niels Lyngsø, trans. from the Danish, Bookthug, Toronto (2005)

Totem, APR (2007)
Winner of the *American Poetry Review* / Honickman First Book Prize

DIGEST
Gregory Pardlo

Four Way Books
Tribeca

Please direct all inquiries to:
Editorial Office
Four Way Books
POB 535, Village Station
New York, NY 10014
www.fourwaybooks.com

Library of Congress Cataloging-in-Publication Data

Pardlo, Gregory, author.
[Poems. Selections]
Digest / Gregory Pardlo.
pages cm
ISBN 978-1-935536-50-5 (pbk. : alk. paper)
I. Title.
PS3616.A737A6 2014
811'.6--dc23
          2014011291

2nd printing, 2015

This book is manufactured in the United States of America and printed on acid-free paper.

Four Way Books is a not-for-profit literary press. We are grateful for the assistance
we receive from individual donors, public arts agencies, and private foundations.

This publication is made possible with public funds from the National Endowment for the Arts

NYSCA

and from the New York State Council on the Arts, a state agency

and from the Jerome Foundation.

[clmp]

We are a proud member of the Council of Literary Magazines and Presses.

Distributed by University Press of New England
One Court Street, Lebanon, NH 03766

Contents

The Clinamen Improvisations

Notes

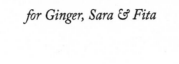

for Ginger, Sara & Fita

Written by Himself

I was born in minutes in a roadside kitchen a skillet
whispering my name. I was born to rainwater and lye;
I was born across the river where I
was borrowed with clothespins, a harrow tooth,
broadsides sewn in my shoes. I returned, though
it please you, through no fault of my own,
pockets filled with coffee grounds and eggshells.
I was born still and superstitious; I bore an unexpected burden.
I gave birth, I gave blessing, I gave rise to suspicion.
I was born abandoned outdoors in the heat-shaped air,
air drifting like spirits and old windows.
I was born a fraction and a cipher and a ledger entry;
I was an index of first lines when I was born.
I was born waist-deep stubborn in the water crying
              ain't I a woman and a brother I was born
to this hall of mirrors, this horror story I was
born with a prologue of references, pursued
by mosquitoes and thieves, I was born passing
off the problem of the twentieth century: I was born.
I read minds before I could read fishes and loaves;
I walked a piece of the way alone before I was born.

Marginalia

for Colin Channer

"sing the Union cause, sing us,/ the poor, the marginal."
—Robert Hayden, "Homage to Paul Robeson"

Preamble

Note the confection of your body
salt on the breeze, the corn-
silk sky. Olmstead's signature
archways and meadows. Kite
strings tensing the load of a saddle-
backed wind. This is Prospect Park,
Brooklyn, where limbs tickle
and jounce as if ice cubes shiver
along the shirtsleeves of evergreens. Pond
water whispers, and the echoes of Yankee
fifes linger in wind and in the shirring jazz
hands of leaves, and those shirts,
the skins, the human retinue converging
on the uneven playing fields. The African
drum and dance circle sways the pignut
tree into a charismatic trance as
Orthodox women walk powerfully by, jogging
shoes blinking beneath the billows of their
skirts, children rollerblading, trailing
tzitzits. Take heart in the percussion
structuring the distance like prophetic
weather, a shelter of vibrations:
the last conga note a bolt tapped into
the day's doorframe and you are no less,
no more home here than in the corridors

4

you return to in your dreams. Illusory,
altogether babel-fractured, a single word
from you might bring the verdant fun-house
down. Listen like a safecracker, navigate
the intricate ruptures by ear: the Latin
patois of picnickers, the Slavic tongues
of lovers replacing your mouth with self-
conscious silence. You are Caliban
and Crusoe, perpetual stranger with a fork
in the socket of life's livid grid,
stunned and bewildered at the frank
intrusion of the mosquito on the hairless
back of your hand. You are stranded
at the limit, extremity and restriction,
jealous for that elusive—the domestic, yes,
you're thinking: not the brick and mortar, but
the quickening backfill of belonging, the stranger-
facing, the neighbor-knowing confidence and ease
with the ripple that diminishes as it extends
over the vast potential of immovable thirst.
You are home now, outsider, for what that's worth.

Problemata

In the *Preamble*, Gouverneur Morris refers, poetically,
to the "domestic tranquility" shattered by rebelling
veterans who, unable to pay mounting war taxes, confronted
the state for having seized their homes. They argued
their point with bayonets fixed to their flintlock rifles. Point being
that blood should have been enough, as it was in their barter
economy, to square their debt in the Revolution.
Morris could not abide an economy that imagined exchange
in such discrete terms. For him, every shilling appraised on an altar
of speculative devotions, every home subject to the metaphoric
notion of home, the value of tranquility proportionate
to the power one has to gerrymander the metaphor.

Consider the dear evangelists who canvass our homes
Saturday mornings, who share their pamphlets and good
words, their domestic concerns swelling with their
longing for the fellowship of us. Spinoza gives us
this reason not to opt off of their call lists: *The good
which a man desires for himself and loves, he will love
more constantly if he sees that others love it also;
he will therefore endeavor that others should love it also.*
Be tolerant of their attention, their pursuit of agape,
a planet-sized chip they bear on their shoulders
from house to house, door to door, welcome
or not, blessing whatever they find inside.

I finally friended my brother.
It may be we will never
speak again. Why speak
when we have this crystal ball
through which
to judge one another's lives?
I imagine this is what
the afterlife will be like.
I'm ghost, we say
instead of goodbye.

It is nearly July in Brooklyn and already
the fireworks from Chinatown warehouses
are bursting in stellar fluorescence like tinsel-tied
dreadlocks above the Bushwick tenements and the brownstone
blocks of Bed-Stuy now littered with the skittering
décollage of wrappers exploded across blacktops and handball
courts, playgrounds and sidewalks knuckled by tree roots.
My neighbor's teenaged boys argue who possesses the greatest
patriotism. Just as pit bulls chained to their fists imply
their roughly domesticated manhood,
they seek to demonstrate their patriotism with bottle
rockets, spinners, petards, these household paraphernalia of war.
The competition is vigorous, draws spectators and blood.
When the smoke clears, no charges
are filed. We neighbors waver distractedly a moment
before tracing our paths back into our quiet homes.

Problema 1

Because Venus lifted the Rosewater Dish like a shield
in the sun the graying father of two swatted a juggle
of balls against a playground wall that had been graffitied
for an episode of *Law & Order* set in the hood.
The desiccated catgut of his racquet strummed
like a junkyard harp with each gouty ground stroke.
A muscle fire stoked to warm the bagpipes in his chest.
Like a waft of charcoal in the park, there came to him
thought of the bargain implied in God's command
to Abraham. Not unlike Robert Johnson's deal
at the crossroads or Gauguin's pricey escape from
the obscurity of the middle class, these appeals
to the brute motives of the blood, mortal
insecurity seeking relief in the barter for fertility,
which is to say, fame. This was the mind of the man
as he stiffened and hid his wind in a falsely barreling
chest, setting out to retrieve what may have seemed
portentous—a citrine moon descending
on the shirtless men playing handball
on the opposite court, an intrusion like a cell phone
ringing in Alice Tully Hall. Their annoyance was muted
but palpable for they, too, were performing
the ritual of their devotions. What he wouldn't give to hear,
like a nest of hungering chicks, his flock, the epochal
cry of thousands in the stadium around Centre Court,
his name on the wind. Perhaps he'd swap it all for the boy
he once was, the future altered, and follow
some stellar herald, righteousness and treason
arcing in his mind like a halo, to risk a life
he could only begin to imagine.

Problema 2

"My Father they have killed me."
            —Chinua Achebe

Consider throwing the baby from the window a figure
of speech barely reaching across the fence separating
expression from intent. *For all our sake*, I tell my wife,
I'm going to throw the baby out the window now,
as I rise from the sofa in response to the midnight
wail of another footie uprising heard among
the moans and whines of our neighbors' appliances
and the various alarms of the city's eternal self-soothing.
The ancient hardwood floor in the bedroom upstairs
groaning under thirty-pound footsteps for the fourth time
tonight. It is nearly July in Brooklyn. Windows are open.
Consider the neighbors grimacing, pillowing
their ears against the little one's battle cry.

Because I am teaching Euripides in the fall, I am
reading him now between commercial breaks, and
imagining far-flung Brooklyn quorumed in the armories
and in streets beneath the gingkoes and buttonwoods,
crowds gathered to mandate I quiet my lamb eternally.
What if my neighbors read my hyperbole as oath, made me
keep my word? Who would I betray? Would I smuggle
my mewling daughter to Canada, flee this land? I do love
Brooklyn so. I have lent a neighborly ear to elderly
West Indians on the B44 from Bed-Stuy to Flatbush.
Heard them lament Yankee reluctance to use
old-country discipline, which, they claim, is the only real
solution to this climate of "gang foolery." Spanking. Yes.
The sacramental rod tanning backsides of the elect few,
a ritual hazing to appease the divinity of the unknowable
and omnipresent urban populace. Consider the vanity
of sacrifice, the paper tiger of blind devotion fanning

11

the dander of a timid hand. Consider Agamemnon,
victim of pride and contagion, raising that hand
against his child at Aulis, the inexorable machinery of tribalism
grinding away the primacy of paternal love. Beware the prophet,
the genie, the divine stranger who, with a wink, unmasks your
arrogant self-images, who finds the harmonic note that gathers
your most discordant emotions toward the mute
accumulation of will. *What I do this night
I do for you, Brooklyn*, I offer,
as the banister whimpers beneath my trembling hand.

Problema 3

The Fulton St. Foodtown is playing Motown and I'm surprised
at how quickly my daughter picks up the tune. And soon
the two of us, plowing rows of goods steeped in fructose
under light thick as corn oil, are singing *Baby,*
I need your lovin', unconscious of the lyrics' foreboding.
My happy child riding high in the shopping cart as if she's
cruising the polished aisles on a tractor laden with imperishable
foodstuffs. Her cornball father enthusiastically prompting
with spins and flourishes and the double-barrel fingers
of the gunslinger's pose. But we hear it as we round the rice
and Goya aisle, that other music, the familiar exchange of anger,
the war drums of parent and child. The boy wants, what, to be
carried? to eat the snacks right from his mother's basket?
What does it matter, he is making a scene. With no self-interest
beyond the pleasure of replacing wonder with wonder, my daughter
asks me to name the boy's offense. I offer to buy her ice cream.
How can I admit recognizing the portrait of fear the mother's face
performs, the inherited terror of non-conformity frosted with the fear
of being thought disrespected by, or lacking the will to discipline,
one's child? How can I account for both the cultural and the inter-
cultural? The boy's cries rising like hosannas as the mother's purse
falls from her shoulder. Her missed step from the ledge
of one of her stilted heels, passion loosed with each displaced
hairpin. His little jacket bunched at the collar where she has worked
the marionette. Later, when I'm placing groceries on the conveyor
belt and it is clear I've forgotten the ice cream, my daughter
tries her hand at this new algorithm of love, each word
punctuated by her little fist: *boy*, she commands, *didn't I tell you?*

Problema 4

At thirteen I asked my father for a tattoo.
I might as well have asked for a bar mitzvah.
He said I had no right to alter the body
he gave me. Aping what little of Marx I learned
from the sisters down the street who wore torn
black stockings with Doc Martens, I said
I was a man because I could claim my body
and the value of its labor. This meant I could
adorn it or dispose of it as I chose. Tattoos,
my father said, are like children: have one,
you'll want another. I knew there was a connection
between the decorated body and reproduction.
This is why I wanted a tattoo. Yet I reasoned,
not in so many words, his analogy only held
in the case of possession, i.e., I possess my body,
but can not possess my children. His laughter
was my first lesson in the human Ponzi
scheme of paternalism, the self-electing
indenture to the promise of material inheritance,
men claiming a hollow authority because,
simply, their fathers had claimed
a hollow authority. Knowing I had little
idea as to what my proposed tattoo might
resemble, my father sent me to my room
to sketch it using the pastels he had given me
for Christmas. Based on his critique, he said,
he would consider my request. But he had
already taken the shine from my swagger.
How can I beautify what I do not possess
and call it anything but graffiti? Chris Rock says
my first job is to keep my daughter

14

off the pole. Whether or not I agree with him,
I get his point. As a father myself
I now see every mutinous claim of independence
as the first steps toward my sweet pea's
falling in with a bad crowd. Richard Pryor
says we are bound to fuck up our kids
one way or another. My father would
split the difference: *I made you*, he'd say,
I can un-make you, and make another one
just like you.

Attachment: Atlantic City Pimp

Left of the @ sign the email address
was ethnically gendered with the nonce
noun *sistah*, which, I have to confess,

I scoffed at, thinking it was from some self-
discovering student of mine, before realizing it was
my aunt who sent the jpeg from her cell

phone. My aunt who doesn't mind
a bit of shell if it means getting all the crabmeat,
who is known to only leave behind

enough of a tip to shame the wait staff
for their inattention. The subject line read:
"AC Pimp" as if her painted nails and belly laugh

made her expert in the fauna of pimps, a soul-stirred
savant of things cold-blooded. As if she could
divine an ivory handled Derringer holstered

at his breast icing the steel heart cognate
to the gun, that twin ventriloquist of tinder
and sulfur dust, that rhythmic and delicate

organ pumping like a fist that has a knack
for snake eyes and the superfluity of bruises
that follow every spaghetti-strapped back-

talker's doubt. She must have thought
she'd reached her brother, my father, who harbors
like a gold molar a taste for robin egg and mauve

pocket squares, a flourish of trim, a hand-stitch,
lapels check striped and foreshortened
like tyrannosaurus arms and ostrich

print Stacy Adams to match. The modest,
feathered derby contrasting all those boas
festooning street lamps and mail boxes.

But my aunt is no mere expert.
 "AC" may have been a random tag,
but that word "Pimp" bore the import

of all us do-wrong men. She was, in effect,
signifying—the kind of humor that waters
the eye, the doubletalk, the shadow dialect.

Like her spite-tinged smile at a bridal
shower, her patina of derision enlivened
the photo. My aunt, who refuses to settle

for a man less Christian than she is finds
everywhere despicable men. Hence the dozens
via email, the critique, like a razor inside

a roll of twenties, the currency
of our vengeance economy. Perhaps
there was an untroubled sea

just beyond the garish casinos behind him,
a stilt-walker or mime outside the frame,
a carnival and boardwalk where the horizon

would be, and a tour bus full of people waving.
Of all the images that might speak to something
inside her, this was the one she found worth saving.

Corrective Lenses: Creative Reading and (Recon)textual/ization

A text dropped in the brain's pail rattles the way astrophysicists say they can hear the birth of time tuning the salt rim of Saturn. For example, *Finnegan's Wake*. For example, horoscopes, and little notes folded into cookies. The Society of Prophetic Archeologists argues all arguments are subject to confirmation bias. In this course we will venerate the subjective mind, or rather, examine how subject/ object share the fuzzy circumference of a lone spotlight beneath the proscenium arch. There is no reliable narrator. For example, tea leaves or cloudbursts in the shape of ladybirds. We will interrogate the cagey and shifting sign in order to coerce all its false confessions. We will learn to project our backslashes to snatch a suffix like the fake mustache of an incognito, impose parentheses to ironize our dependence on convention. Because there are no valid means of assessment students are encouraged to assign their own grade upon registration. Any book will do: phone, face, match, bank. We will set course across wastelands of difficult punchlines under bad signs to flush the comic truth like what? a flock of starlings? a dime bag ? while we pretend a grasp of subtleties as they spiral sparkshowers like a Chinese New Year, red, gold, red, gold, red, gold.

Four Improvisations on Ursa Corregidora

after Gayl Jones

My husband Mutt backhanded me down the fire
escape out back a blues bar called *Happy's*. Nothing
holds a family together like irony and a grudge.
Depends on what you call family. What's left now
of the generation I hadn't known I made is just a scar
squoze shut like a mouth that won't eat, a score
where doctors had to retrieve the fetus, its tub
and my plumbing altogether. Now I'm soundproof,
and now I'm forever hollow as a plaster statue.
Just as I can't go back to where my mothers cast
me out to flatter their memories chiming, echoing,
braiding the wind with their eccentric melody, Mutt
can't come back to me no more. I can picture him though
harassing the shadows of my voice, drunk as a judge.

My husband Mutt handled the hose that doused the fire,
the reason I can't make babies. I've claimed the blues
is a current like electricity, but mine was a combustion
engine cutting shapes out of noise. Lying at the bottom
of those stairs I could already feel my machine slipping
into pictures of still water. I began swallowing water-
melon seeds by the handful hoping something take root:
a vine, a silence. I was reborn at the crime scene;
I survived the rent in time to look back on it squeezing
shut like a fist. A refrain: echolalia: bad penny: menses.
Evidence of a pattern we are determined to reveal
when we find ourselves standing before the judge.
Evidence of the devil we're determined to reveal
when we're testifying for the jury and the judge.

My husband Mutt stared back down the barrel of his years,
came up loaded and hapless. I was determined
to take him in spite of my history, to refrain from adding
to the pattern emerging from the rueful chorus: my mothers
cast me as amanuensis to record their versions
of the crime. Once upon a time means once and for always
and for wherever you are and now I'm singing blues
in a bar revealing as much skin as you should
be willing to reveal when you pouring your seed
into the electric element. We are given two names:
one to work like witness protection, and one to carry
mechanically to the grave. I never took my husband's name.
I imagine that would be as useful as a newspaper covering
my head in the rain. Useful as letting my eyes be the judge.

My husband Mutt handed me back all the love he felt
I had failed to give him. That's saying something close
to nothing. "Do nothing til you hear from me," he said,
and smiled. Whoever owns these blues is a matter
of some debate. The story of my people unfolds
each day like a newspaper detailing the catechism
that connects me to history: *Are you hurt?* Yes, I am
the hurt, the silent mouth is the barter. *What's a husband
good for?* Seed money. Generations working the fields. *Why
do we make dreams?* A little ritual. A little lining for the purse.
Each song is a number of the seven veils: each number is
a revelation of skin measuring degrees of distance from
the crime and from the guilt of the crime. Corregidora:
as much kin as we're willing to reveal lest we be judged.

Copyright

Paul Green
Of course I know the story of the scorpion
and the frog. I've known Biggers all my life.
I've cast down my buckets where I've stood
with them, working shoulder to shoulder,
our bodies forming a double helix in the fields. And
when the mob came for Dick didn't I sit anyways
outside his quarters all night like a jailhouse lawyer,
him ignorant of the nature of his custody?
It was me who kept the townsmen at bay after he
provoked them. My cousin among them
had watched him grin and wheedle,
consort with white people carelessly, our naïve
and guileless women, at the civil gathering where
he was my ward. And later, because of me,
his offense went unanswered, un-atoned.
I know the hearts of men are governed
by the endowments of nature. As some children
are faithful. Some are made to obey.

Charles Leavell
First I had to corner the boy
in a thicket of print.
He tried to make my happy darky
dangerous, make my darky
an idea that I couldn't bear to swallow. So
I made him a hothouse flower, writing, *His hunched
shoulders and long, sinewy arms that dangle
almost to his knees*, but warned
readers that Nixon, the "Brick
Slayer," as I christened him,

had none of the charm of speech
or manner that is characteristic of so many
southern darkies. I am a gentle man.
He is very black—almost pure Negro. Withal,
I had to cleave that slate with first words, in order
to get at him, get the nature right, and I
could almost hear stone sing
like the brick
he used to beat the white woman
who discovered him, that June day in '38,
bagging her Philco radio—as if it were
me doing the slaying.

Richard Wright
One quarter argument two
quarters confession. I engender
my experience in the characters
and they thrive; for the balance
I tracked Robert Nixon, so-called
"Brick Slayer," through rows
and columns, finding him breathing
in the margins of the *Chicago Tribune.*
I loved that boy like redemption
loves a sinner and saw in him
the mute pronouncements of the proletariat,
mutiny on the Potemkin. No wonder I
was reluctant to ditch the script I wrote
with Paul Green, that playwright
accused of being a lover of the down-
trodden. Much as I wished to avoid
controversy, when Welles demanded

a Bigger without dream sequences, without
singing, for the Broadway production,
I sighed relief. I knew I had to protect
my creation from the caustic
ministrations of Southern sensibility.
By North Star or candlelight, by necessity,
I had to spirit him away.

Robert Nixon
More crucial than surveillance in the round
house of corrections is the being
watched the prisoner faces raising hairs on the ears.
Like the sun's warmth on the back recognized as light,
recognized as presence. White noise.
The confinement of plain sight. The vertiginous spin
siphoning off the will to question, to doubt,
g-forces pinning back the cheeks, inmates
reduced to images affixed by the weight of the guard's
transparent eyeball, the unreasoning stump of muscle
itself imprisoned like the figures stenciled on an urn.

Renaissance Man

after Ralph Ellison

Born standing, Rinehart. Shafts of heat,
lightning conceived him. Blink,
and he's a curl of smoke on the flashpoint,
the residue of his momentary need.
Here is the rind, here is the unexplainable
heart, the parts, the particles. A shape
shifter, a trick of the eye inside the living
tableau, he's whatever he wants
you to see. Deacon, daddy-o, ·
doctor, Demosthenes. The ever
receding horizon in the book of Monopolated power
and light. Book of the humble easing
the veil from his own shoulders. Sewage
and the lumpen in an estuary of beer
carts and dead revolutionaries hatched this
one-man cast of double agents.

Duplicity spreads, like a roll of gauze, to mask
the face beneath the haberdasher's brim of him who is
the incarnate pronoun, who is willing, if necessary,
to be the errant wrench, the ghost in the gear box
of a grandfather clock setting the race back
to all the electrified carpets, fighting for power and light,
willing to venture the logic of the black
black-faced minstrel, the nobility of the hobo and the rodeo
clown, the carnival ride of irony called
the black body. If he'd paint an eye on the rusty
palm of his hand he'd find Rinehart's
thrift vision in a network of hep sensibility.
The cradles of the skull would screen the flipped images
of Rinehart's limitless industry behind those dark

lenses looted from a Harlem pharmacy. Yet he
must find Rinehart—frisking himself
as if looking for a matchbook, a set of keys—
tangibly, the man, the ontological
gangster, the enigma mirrored in a stranger's eye.

Shades of Green: Envy and Enmity in the American Cultural Imaginary

Images of the stud and the buck have an amorously crafted resonance burnished by cultural anxieties, an addict's logic toward the habit they place in the mind and the mysteries we lay at their feet. This course will begin by focusing on models represented in the 1994 Charles Russell film, *The Mask*, and Ang Lee's 2003 *The Hulk*. The mojo and the genetic regression, the hyper-sexuality and the rage: these qualities are thrust and airbrushed onto the bacchic body of the Other, as we fantasize our repression of them in ourselves, the unquiet threat of psychosomatic greening; a silk garrote, an onanistic envy of the Other's capacity for release; a monumental iconography of the hermetical black box of the brain. While we might be tempted to reduce these types to the pat dichotomy of comedy and tragedy, this course will examine the ways in which there is but one mask, a Janus-faced cleavage of thou art and thus am I, our goat-sung desires adrift in the wilderness, our telltale passions pulsing beneath the tulips and gladiolas in a mildewed hatbox (the act of masking triumphal and deadly), trembling the bulb on its stem.

Copenhagen, 1991

As adversaries we made good
lovers, made heat where there was little
to hold in common but youth and wanderlust
until I found her with a former valentine reclining
under skyrockets of wilted mistletoe,
where the yuletide ebbed and "Auld Lang Syne"
wheezed away on chariots of snow.
My buckling knees upturned a crate of Clementines
which drummed a stumblehearted rhythm
across the snowcrusted cobbles to her feet.

Yellow gloves to my elbows in the suds
at *Spiseloppen*, an eatery for hippies
and bikers from Pusher Street who tipped me
with blocks of hash. The waitress first palmed
the bits of sintered brick like deposit slips
at the window where I had cried
Klare! then shuffled trays of pint glasses
and flatware in water blued by sanitizing tablets,
and I waved a latex thanks to the flame-haired socialists
who toasted me as they toasted the chefs as well.

                    Like a cat on pine
needles, I danced the waitress out to smoke
a chillum with the piano man. Much of an hour.
Who could interrupt her stunning
a parked window with her pout, soothing wrinkles
from her apron? Damp flame with a burnt Prince
Light behind my ear, I began to mimic liquid
and the moment's departure like crowds ungathering,
the waitress leading me kittenish and heart-

starved across cold cobble in the rawboned motif
of a morning. I was the only chirping; songlets
and the eking moon, throat bells keening, I moved
toward her mouth. Stuffed tiger, she said,
I will carry you home in my teeth.

Ghosts in the Machine: Synergy and the Dialogic System

Self-effacing, the number zero stands austere, a window onto Nature's abhorrent force, a hyperborean rebuke to the tropic heat of being. We might say zero is the perfection of affect, round as a pucker it dallies, dispassionate, for a kiss. In this course, we will observe our stalwart and lonely hero, zero, and its intercourse with the number one or, what Nietzsche refers to as "Dionysiac rapture," the "vision of mystical Oneness" symbolizing the root assertion of self-surrender: *yes*. And we will study how this primordial union begets the mystery of Zeno's arrow stitching the sky across a battlefield, or begets the way sweet nothings from a random-dialing jailhouse phone might morbidly prick the pulse. We will consider the connotative spark rattling like a pinball in the void between two bumpers of denotation, overloading the light bulb above our heads, or worse, animating anxieties strapped to the gurney within. That one hand clapping, for example. For example, the call is coming from inside the house.

Palling Around

He heard in curtains of sleet cleaving
from magnolia leaves encrypted Aztec
frequencies, he said. When the sun
god liquors loose each ashen tongue
the planet tattles. We are advised
to listen: this he'd grunt to signal his

dwindling fuse and the bartender would
show him the door. In his honor I tune
my form to the emanations of this vibrant
life: Either someone's dropped a blue
coin and I've picked up the murmur of its
ribs—a quarter kiltering beneath the blond

brick arcade of the whispering gallery
at Grand Central—or someone's table
is ready. No matter that I set my phone
to airplane while I thumb these lines, I can
still be reached by tender thought: a dirgeful
brass cortège stirs the ear inside my chest.

The man has passed. I got the text today,
and now feel at least obliged to observe
silence. Observe this café thick with humid
bodies, mugs wafting florets of breath, steam
revealing patterns in the glassy chatter.
For that he is a phantasm rumoring now

a timeless doom, quiet as the carousel
of a partial print. For that he is finally
transcendent. For that we convened for

drinks by some clockwork of urban chance
each week, my year adrift in the East Village.
For that I renounced him, and now regret

having done so. For that I vibed with his
passions—more, the deeper we reached in
our cups, rifling our mind's files for magical
thinking and secrets in our blood's chemical
record. I've traveled years through boot-black
redactions of thought to find his apparition

greet me with a raised fist in the dream of a
leather trench coat that crunches like gravetop
snow, dream of the self-schooled on secondary
sources. He hung a cardboard pyramid to cover
the bed in which he slept and quested visions
toward the headwaters of paranoia: nightsweats

of tar, drumbeats marooned in the distant hills,
Legba tapping his cane on the edge of sanity.
If you see something. What a fear of hobgoblins
and philistines can blind our better senses.
At the table beside me children play mosquito
tones they say are there, but I am unable to hear.

Raisin

I dragged my twelve-year-old cousin
to see the Broadway production of *A Raisin
in the Sun* because the hip-hop mogul
and rapping bachelor, Diddy, played
the starring role. An aspiring rapper gave
my cousin his last name and the occasional child
support so I thought the boy would geek to see a pop
hero in the flesh as Walter Lee. My wife was newly
pregnant, and I was rehearsing, like Diddy
swapping fictions, surrendering his manicured
thug persona for a more domestic performance.
My cousin mostly yawned throughout the play.
Except the moment Walter Lee's tween son stiffened
on stage, as if rapt by the sound of a roulette ball.
Scene: *No one breathes as Walter Lee vacillates,
uncertain of obsequity or indignation after Lindner offers
to buy the family out of the house they've purchased
in the all-white suburb. Walter might kneel to accept,
but he senses the tension in his son's gaze.* I was thinking,
for real though, what would Diddy do? "Get rich
or die trying," 50 Cent would tell us. But my father would
sing like Ricky Scaggs, "Don't get above your raisin',"
when as a kid I vowed to be a bigger man than him.
That oppressive fruit dropped heavy as a medicine
ball in my lap meant to check my ego, and I imagined
generations wimpling in succession like the conga
marching raisins that sang Marvin's hit song. Silly,
I know. Outside the theater, my cousin told me
when Diddy was two, they found his hustler dad
draping a steering wheel in Central Park,
a bullet in his head. I shared what I knew of dreams

deferred and Marvin Gaye. (When asked if he loved
his son, Marvin Sr. answered, "Let's just say I didn't
dislike him.") Beneath the bling of many billion
diodes I walked beside the boy through Times Square
as if anticipating a magic curtain that would rise,
but only one of us would get to take a bow.

Philadelphia, Negro

Alien-faced patriot in my father's mirrored aviators
that reflected a mind full of cloud
keloids, the contrails of Blue Angels in formation
miles above the campered fields of Willow Grove
where I heard them clear as construction paper slowly
tearing as they plumbed close enough I could nearly see
flyboys saluting the tiny flag I shook in their wakes,
I visored back with pride, sitting aloft dad's shoulders,
my salute a reflex ebbing toward ground crews in jumpsuits
executing orchestral movements with light. The bicentennial
crocheted the nation with the masts of tall ships and twelve-foot
Uncle Sams but at year's end my innocence dislodged
like a powdered wig as I witnessed the first installment
of *Roots*. The TV series appeared like a galleon on the horizon
and put me in touch with all twelve angry tines of the fist
pick my father kept on his dresser next to cufflinks
and his Texas Instruments LED watch. I was not in the market
for a history to pad my hands like fat leather mittens. A kind
of religion to make sense of a past mysterious as basements
with upholstered wet bars and blacklight velvet panthers, maybe,
but as such a youngster I thought every American a Philadelphia
Negro, blue-eyed soulsters and southpaws alike getting
strong now, mounting the art museum steps together
like children swept up in Elton's freedom from Fern Rock
to Veterans Stadium, endorphins clanging like liberty-
themed tourist trolleys unloading outside the Penn Relays,
a temporal echo, an offspring, of Mexico City where Tommie
Smith and John Carlos made a human kinara with the human
rights salute while my father scaled the Summit
Avenue street sign at the edge of his lawn holding a bomb
pop that bled tricolor ice down his elbow as he raised it like

Ultraman's Beta Capsule in flight from a police K9 used to
terrorize suspicious kids. Your dad would be mortified too
if he knew you borrowed such overheard records of oppression
to rationalize casting yourself as a revolutionary American
fourth-grader even though, like America, your father never lifted
your purple infant butt proudly into the swaddling of starlight
to tell the heavens to "behold: the only thing greater
than yourself." And like America, his fist only rose on occasion,
graceful, impassioned, as if imitating Arthur Ashe's balletic serve,
so that you almost forgot you were in its way.

The Conatus Improvisations

Heraclitus: *We cannot know the water, but only its perpetual movement.*

Overheating cannot be blamed on a faulty idiot light.
The car in crisis, beached on the roadside and pouring
steam from its blowhole as you watch the rain melt
the windshield, the perfect screen for projecting a fantasy
dissolve that begins with your jalopy dropped from a barge
to be eaten by the reef like a dive site. An hour earlier this bell
jar hummed and clunkered as it sluiced through vacuum
tubes lining the riverbed from Manhattan to Hoboken,
the interstate peace pipes which lead to the suburban
drive-thru bank window where you hand-deliver your
savings to creditors. You think of self-sabotage, dirigibles
bursting the sky in newsreels over Lakehurst, flaming like
immolating monks. Our machines merely echo our bodies'
disposition: your desire for the tellers to leave their tanks
and swim to your rescue, pretty as new money floating
ghostly outside the car window as the last pockets of air
pinch off and the water gently closes over your head.

St. Augustine: *If no one asks me, I know what it is. If I wish to explain it to him who asks me, I do not know.*

Prince calls it *little* because he imagines a woman's body
waist up, the rest Corvette, which is French for a sort of girlie
warship, a chimerical twist on the Freudian cockpit. Who
wouldn't want a belly button for a windshield? All us baby
ball turret gunners would submit to mother love as long as we
were allowed the illusion that we commanded the vessel. This
may be why we give them names like Bessy and Lila Mae,
but our cars are more prosthesis than portmanteau. We say
horses that muscle and gun, but idle next to one and hear
its sputtering, Promethean delirium like a hound's
twitching dream of dogfights in biplanes that strafe
the velvet sky with the leathery helmets of their little red
barons. We would have swooped the oil fields where pilot
lights burned like Zippos at a rock concert to safeguard our
memories of weekends washing father's Vette, fearing both its
pliant fire and our need to ride in pursuit of some unconscious
joy, certain only that we'd know it if it ever could be found.

Boethius: *The creator moves the slowest bodies and halts those that are too fast, brings back to the right path those which have strayed.*

Even Virgin Mary couldn't compete with the miracles
performed on dashboards by GPS devices that summon
the heavens for guidance instead of forgiveness. Instead of
blessing we want clairvoyance and the dust bursts of angels
and demons appearing on our shoulders, though we know
they may only goad us into leading some high- or low-speed
chase while America tunes in at home, their eyes in the skies.
Used to be the battle of getting there was indeed a tortoise and
hare proposition full of K-turns in strangers' driveways, but our
omniscient technology has made speed obsolete. Who needs to
hurry when we have a hivemind of newsfeeds, can discern death's
thumbprint in the marrow of a bone and engineer children who
are elegant and fleet? In the end, James Dean couldn't outrun
a glacier. Just as the slowest floes preyed timelessly on dinosaurs
and shat their bones, our rockets now fold the speckled
firmament to take orbit on the shoulders of eternity where they
may fill the creator's ears with our mortal doubts and provocations.

Aquinas: *The mover gives what he has to the one who is moved in that it causes him to be in motion.*

Jumping often refers to something you'd rather not
get involved in, but when you've left the parking
lights on overnight, a jump can mean the difference
between being employed and not. Worse than having
to buy a swipe from a stranger on the bus is having to flag
a neighbor for a jump. People willing to defibrillate
flatlining cars on ice scraper mornings are like organ
donors and subway heroes. For karma like that you need
a Winnebago covered with solar panels sprouting a fountain
of jumper cables so you can spend your day suckling
weary vehicles like an electric wet nurse. By your example,
thugs would soon measure their cred by a tattooed lightning
bolt under the eye to symbolize each battery they have
sprung back to life. Soon gangs will jump-in initiates one
toothy clamp at a time, and civilians will jump all over each
other with reciprocal gifts and hugs, finding power where
power is given, a residual lifting of the spirits in the act.

Occam: *Every body has an impetus which allows it to continue to move. Being moved is passing from potential to the act.*

You often size up the random demographic holiday
traffic makes hoping to see yourself inside a picture bigger
than the neighborhood you know. But the knots of cars
strung in rows like Incan quipu ordain your destination for
they script your possibilities in the Nielsen lingo, abstracted
from ad copy instead of the tangible planet. So who is really
driving the soapbox you find transporting your thoughts while
you inch the highway like the Pope's bubble-mobile? Lines at
the toll plaza are a poem where you idle in this way, mindless
as Sonny Corleone. Every procession ends in a funeral. Think
of the chain gang of reindeer and the tiny hands making toys
in Santa's *maquilas*. Will you spend the whole poem reading
bumpers and vanity plates, concerned how they outpace you?
At the end of this poem full of furtive glances will you count
yourself among the seers or the seen? No one sees you sleeping
but your wife, and for her you thought of nothing. Look how little
you give of yourself. How little of yourself you have been given.

Gassendi: *ambulo ergo sum.*

We labor to maintain them in the macadam fields around
Pep Boys, where legs dangle from the maw of upraised hoods
like tailfins draping a pelican's beak. We can say about cars
what Jefferson said about slavery when seeking pity for his
hardships. "Like holding a wolf by the ears." Talk about
awkward. Yet it's for domesticating horses that he charges
Europeans with "the degeneracy of the human body." Perhaps
we are all, like him, exhausted by our compulsion to be free
from carrying our weight, human to heap our load on some other
burdensome body we've subordinated to our sloth. Who could go
on schlepping the lanes flanking Eastern Parkway beneath plane
trees as trumpets from dollar vans blow Dixie? Few haven't caved
to the runagate's dream of those chariots come to carry us home.
Hasidim fill the streets Saturdays with ambling demonstrations
of civil-resistance. James Meredith trod a shoulder in Mississippi
to be free. We may all go someday Pan-like marching, transported
by the rapturous clopping of the only two hooves we can master.

ZoSo

Those hammer-ons on *Over the Hills* made my fingers bleed.
That is, my devotion to their shapes made my fingers bleed.

Child of Crowley, Bukka White, paddling hips across the stage.
Time's architect, sketch blueprints lesser innovators read.

Sight the neck like a rifle barrel. Diagnose the truss rod sound.
Let's caress the fretwork, inlays pearl and filigreed.

Contracts offer details juke growlers shrug off like sheet music.
"How much," they only want to know, "am I *guaranteed*?"

On the frontiers of sound we are nocturnal, we move in shivers,
we watch bobcats, as night-blooming cereus lingers, feed.

My mind is a fuzz box today. Hellhound's got my scent, cornered me
in Room 12-B with the hangman's disposition whiskey drinkers need.

The left hand's a gyromantic dancer, sinister. The cat's cradle
of tablature captures the dragonfly's hover, its speed.

At fourteen I walked the rivulets. A pilgrimage. Late harvest.
I cut my teeth on a washtub bass line shimmering like a centipede.

Spirits filled burn piles on the beach. Smoke and salt infused
the fuselage that hummed the lunar music six strings received.

Shoulda quit you on the shoulder, G, singing backward alphabets
of sky. Fingerprinted, you thought they made your fingers bleed.

Alienation Effects

1

According to conventions of detective fiction I fit the description of the "running man." This character must disprove the theory of his guilt before it is made reality. I, however, believe I am beyond redemption, trapped in the maze of these lines, eluding nothing. I am stranded in the semantics between guilt and innocence. But then I wonder, who isn't?

2

The pink bud of her tongue between her capped teeth reminded me of the raccoon I shot by accident with my air rifle as a child. I lifted it from the bloodstained snow, snow falling patiently beyond the trees. Some assume I did not love my wife. I prized her very much. She stepped into my grief with fairy-tale precision. My pity became her.

3

In hospital I convalesced and read the melodrama presented in *Le Figaro*: "On the morning of 16 November, it is alleged, Professor of Philosophy Louis Althusser strangled his wife during what has been ruled a psychotic break." I am not psychotic, though I have indeed killed my wife. She is dead, it's true. Not scuttling between trap doors beneath the stage to reappear to the amazement of my audience. I realize people need explanations. We want the sleight of hand revealed. We want to rationalize, blame, which is a dress rehearsal for justice, that primal illusion.

4

The arrest of a local boy interrupted the last public row I had with Hélène. I don't know. She may have disagreed with me as to whether the menu belonged to a system of menus. That it had a grammar. We maybe quarreled over the waiter's gratuity. I do recall the boy's face as shopkeepers beat him (I was touched by its pathos) in the square outside the restaurant. I briefly wondered what he had done to demand such punishment.

5

What I remember is this: I was massaging her neck, as I often did. As she often asked me to do. She was stiff. It took much effort. *Ma petite chouchoute*, simple girl. Her stress was great. And then, like a child toggling effortlessly between believe and make believe, she was so limber.

6

Who knew such trifling endearments could lead to this? When we were courting I flit my eyelashes against her cheek each morning before she rose to bathe. It became our safe-word, "butterfly." I never once heard her use it.

7

In the Musée d'Orsay, I used to visit Monet's portrait

of his wife on her deathbed. Some would mistake
the painting for an elegy, but it is not the character
of Camille we find moving so much as Monet's
clinical reckoning of charcoal and ice illuminated
by his own tragic consciousness. He creates a fetish
of Camille's death that is simultaneously obscured
by the authority of his expression. Imagine yourself
inside the moment at which my Hélène realized she
was dying, for example. Drape the moment about
you like a duvet. When you *become* Hélène in this
way, losing yourself to the role I've assigned you, in
empathy, we might say, Hélène disappears from view
and mine is the only being you can comprehend.
How different is that from lovemaking?

8

Memory is the science of stasis. The butterfly of time
pinned to the page inert, resistant to everything
but decay. One of my earliest: As always we were
listening to Puccini in my father's house. Warm
bread and marmalade. Taleggio, Anjou. Father
praising with a wink the marriage between cheese
and pears, while handing me a wedge of the fruit I
watched him slice, blade gently resting to crease the
pillow of his thumb. Matte, bulbous nail. Hands
of a pampered gorilla. Beach grass gusting. *Stay
moment, thou art so fair.*

9

Maybe a dozen Vaudeville acts my dreams produced.
I found myself sawing her in half, playing William

Tell with a glass of whiskey on her head, heaving wine bottles like daggers at her body pinned and spinning on a wagon wheel—all socially approved sideshow bits reminiscent of a Fellini film. Through the false bottom of which reality she finally gave me the slip is a mystery to me still.

10

I can see the Dean and his assistant sitting on the embroidered linen of the unmade bed. First to arrive. Their overcoats and fedoras darkened heavy with shadow and the inclement weather. Their wing tips muddy the rug. I can smell the damp must of their clothes, the cloying nicotine sharp against the antiseptic air of the bedroom. All of it. Almost real. They are waiting for an answer. I want to explain I had no motive but they are suspicious, sniffing the air for clues. Detective fiction demands motive. I turn up the heels of my hands, examine them. Empty. They shake their heads no. Give it to us again they say. Start at the beginning. I sigh, unbutton my cuffs. "Gentlemen," I say. "There is nothing hidden in my sleeves."

11

My face now pale and creased as a kabuki player. I ponder my hands that no longer seem hands. *Ma chérie*, your trapezius was rigid as a child's pencil bag. Each morning now alarm clocks shake from my face by the net full and I am helpless to swat them, to hear their brass crescendo against the bedroom walls, falling to the floor in shards. Again, again, again. I would abolish time if I didn't need a space between each word.

12

It could be her estrangement within the family structure would never approximate Mother's, a failure I could not forgive. I pitied them both and in return one of them despised me. The other despised me not enough.

13

Years later, alone now Althusser must refer to himself in the third person in order to feel whole as he shakes the last beads of Armagnac free, and watches the fire fragment through facets of the decanter. Quilt of glass. The fire chokes down another log like a chocolate candy and coughs brightly behind a veil of pipe smoke. He recalls the tasseled lampshade upset on the floor, bulb baking a spot against the velvet-flocked wallpaper. The unmade bed, impression in the sheets like a snow angel.

14

"Monster," she called me, her voice portending the punishment I craved. But she said she'd had enough, and threatened to walk out. Months passed before she vowed to kill herself. Before I knew it, she was insisting that I end her suffering for her, illustrating how I might do it. She broke the contract. She insisted on making me the man of her dreams.

15

One summer at my grandparent's home my nose opened to the world from which Mother had otherwise protected me: reek of the gingko fruits underfoot, horseshit and the estrus of beasts in the surrounding wood. The chanterelles like moss-cradled bits of pumpkin husk beside ochre puddles in the wheel ruts of the lowland road. Rainwater scummed in the cistern to the privy, the drowned field mouse I fished from it and pocketed to show Mother.

16

On the morning of 16 November, 1980, Hélène Althusser died dreaming of the proletariat and of the executions of Nazi officers she'd tracked to Mexico. She imagined herself a pistolera, a bandolier bracing her sunburnt breast, small clouds grazing the mesas, the aftertaste of tequila fogging her sinuses.

17

I was not incarcerated in the conventional sense. My days are like unnumbered hash marks on the tumbler of a safe suspended above Hélène snoring in the bed beside me. (It is a dream I know well: ropes groaning against a barn pulley as the safe dodders overhead like an inebriated cloud.) My flat is a kaleidoscope of polished rooms, each one reflecting the same colored flakes of memory spilled over from the room before. Some argue psychiatry is not custody, that I eluded justice. But these scenes are inescapable. These lines I am made to recite each time I feel the presence of an eye in the peephole. My parents, Hélène, teachers, colleagues, the school administrators, my analyst and doctors, the bureaucrats, all are gathered in the wings of memory whispering in collaboration. In this vast production of truth, how can any one of us be singled out for responsibility?

18

What is the point of amusement other than to forestall indifference? Hélène was the Alpha muse, let's say. The others were the sheep I collected to keep her engaged.

19

On the morning of 16 November, 1980, Hélène Althusser died after sieving obscure impressions through the Tarot in her dream: Butterflies cloud the mind of the King of Swords. Lightning strikes the tower, felling the Queen.

20

Your narrator is a dispassionate stenographer, a clerk in the bestiary of his mind offering forensic explanations for the facets of his being. Perhaps she would still be alive had I been a poet. If I had been a poet I might have found the words to enter her emotional consciousness. Care as I may the will is weak and I can't wrap myself in the moment of her passing. Poe says the death of a beautiful woman is the most poetical topic in the world. Are these my only options? Enshrine her in the church of the beautiful or display her in a cage of misogyny? I am no poet. She was no beauty.

21

She was once for me comforting as the music of lakewaves, a berceuse massaging the shore, the water's surface bunching at my knees while Mother called me in from the summer rain. Over the years Hélène had become glacial in her fantasies of vengeance and justice. The more strident her oaths became, the more burlesque I found her performance.

22

Alienation effect, *Verfremdungseffekt*, the so-called distancing effect: the Brechtian alarm that startles us from our narcotic trance under the pendulous tock of dramatic diversions we might easily mistake for the world beyond the curtain of language—the way the bell is struck and a young woman crosses the ring to mark rounds in a bout of fisticuffs, briefly returning us to the vestigial light of truth. The conjurer's illusion exposed, the restoration of justice. I wanted to restore her, snap her out of her brood. Instead she joined the blue brigades of eternal hypnotics, and now I am the one unable to sleep.

23

Cyclops banters with Nobody. Solitude is a negation, an absence I choose, my bride, this vapid companion. She will be my undoing. Do I despise her? I do.

24

On the morning of 16 November, 1980, Hélène Althusser died dreaming fistfuls of red ribbon erupting from the breasts of players in Nazi uniforms and the twilit furnace of the sun setting backstage of the horizon over a charcoal bay, a puff of smoke tangled in gaunt limbs of plum trees in bare bloom, and the unborn weight of sorrow.

25

You want me to be the satanic hero of this little epic, but the facts of my life afford me no redemption, as the form requires. A stage play, a mask, I am merely a curtain of words. I cannot absolve you. I cannot dress your wounds. I can't deliver you, Pardlo. You won't find a hero in all of your books. The figure that haunts you is your own design. Let her go.

26

A thousand ships, their sirens, gendarmes approaching. The men drawn near, hunched and preening, gathering on the power lines and circling above. Does your beautiful and distant mother explain the chronic self-loathing, the match you pretend surprises as you watch it nuzzle into your pinch? And the revelation of her affairs after forty years of marriage in that small South Jersey town of yours, coming as it did in the pall cast by the confession of your own infidelity, is it any consolation, we might ask, to know now that she was starving too? Is that justice?

27

Negation is a structure that humbles most. Could I be the cause of an action that does not follow from the expression of my will, but rather from an illegible and transcendent desire? Could I have had nothing and everything to do with this? You understand, I find accidents fascinating.

28

On the morning of 16 November, 1980, Hélène Althusser died dreaming herself adrift in a swarm of Vichy agents alighting on her shoulders and forearms, entreating games of chance, shimmer of wristwatches lining their trench coats like some lamé out of Klimt. And she darkened to wonder, in the confidence grift of history, who was the mark?

29

I knew all along. Children always know. ˙

837. Wilson, Shurli-Anne Mfumi. <u>Black Pampers: Raising</u> <u>Consciousness in the Post-Nationalist Home</u>. Blacktalk Press, Lawnside, NJ, 1976. 442 pp., illustrator unknown. 10 ½ x 11 7/8".

Want tips for nursery décor? Masks and hieroglyphics, akwaba dolls. Send Raggedy Ann to the trash heap. This tome is a how-to for upwardly mobile black parents beset with the guilt of assimilation. Revealed here are the safetypinnings of the nascent black middleclass, their leafy split-level cribs and infants with Sherman Hemsley hairlines. Of interest are bedtime polemics on the racist derivations of "The Wheels on the Bus." Chapter headings address important questions of the day: How and how soon should you intervene if you suspect your child lacks rhythm? At what age should you begin initiating your little one to the historical memory of slavery? And how ethical is the two-cake solution (one party for classmates, and a second so you can invite the cousins)? Indispensible to collectors for whom Aesop's African origin is no matter of debate will be the gloss and annotation, comprising the bulk of the text, of the lyrics to Stevie Wonder's "Black Man." According to the jacket copy, one of the alternate titles considered was, "What to Expect When You're No Longer Expecting Revolution."

Usual occasional scattered light foxing to interiors; contemporary tree calf exceptional. About-fine condition. $75.00

Prom Lighting with Cummerbund

(after Ed Clark's *Vertical Pink & Blue*)

She says you're not cleaning it up you're just
moving it around and then she swings an orbit
with her hip (a cosmic burlesque) that makes
the air echo broad strokes of her punch-

sodden pirouette. He centers a mental push
broom for balance, aligns it with his sternum,
hears its bristles soughing like a needle stranded
at the label. He imagines this the broom

his uncle plies past rows of gun blue lockers
lined like gutted fish expiring through louvered
gills quiet evenings after school. Before man
measures a dollop of pomade man must have

an idea what a dollop is. Listen, she says, and he
notices her lisp. One dance upright can yield
an easy ticket to an upended sunrise of ethereal
neon and ash. Or it may be the Silk Road you have

in mind, you know, like rhubarb, musk and indigo.
She says red mangroves, their tannins rich in B12, are
a key ingredient in bioluminescent lagoons. And
the question becomes: with such beauty, do we need

the gypsum-flecked ceiling, the creaking parquet floor?
She asks who're you going to follow, me or your
quarreling feet. And it sounds more like a command.
With her drawl, the one he hears as color, smooth as

condensed milk in a double espresso, it sounds like she
is calling him "whore." No one he knows uses such words
that part the curtains of a red light district on his face.
Such ribaldry, he thinks, why blemish it with license?

Chalk Dust on the Air

for Gary Simmons

Our hero explains what lines behave as waves
also behave as particles depending upon the presence
of observers, a market of admirers, etc. Think of sifted
sands Tibetan monks spend months to whisk in minutes:
their attack on nostalgia. Think of Milky Ways of water
damage on the bedroom ceiling. The Apollo module
on the dresser and the Ring Nebula is the blur where
Mom tried to clean expletives crayoned on the wall.
Whorls beyond, imagine a can of Krylon ship-shaped
with braided-rubber-band-propeller roped out to
the nosebleeds in the murk of heaven's hood. The spray
can tags earth's dewy rooftop with synesthetic stars,
foamy scars that welt the blue and melt like meringue
in the dusk, a residue of light in the periphery. Winged seeds
from silver maples at the feet of unshaven sheriffs
offering fists of baby's breath. They smile with cigar stubs
plugging the breach. Renegade lines unleash the hounds,
shake the weight of undressed eyes. When some lines try
to pass for the color behind the color they came in, our hero
attempts no intervention. When he orders the lines disperse,
one sheriff's bullhorn blast unsacks a rain of feathers

Bipolar

(On viewing Charles Caryl Coleman's *View of Vesuvius: Effect 11:25AM* at the Brooklyn Museum)

If every line is a horizon, what when
I have two? One stratus, moody as the treble
string on a lute. Sink the ship that hauls a jagged rune
below the second (field purpling like liver), the ship
untangling its sympathetic plume, perish
from my vaulting ear the sulfurous thought
balloon (the puff sprung like a jack-in-the-box)
and you might think I'm sleeping—though seismic
like a madman on a park bench. The earth trembles
as the 4 train thunders through the tunnels underneath.

No myth, no trigger, no telling what'll set me off.
I don't know what is in me I can't contain. Come,
tell me, which do you think is the line I can't stop crossing?

For Which It Stands

For a flag! I answered facetiously. A flag of tomorrow,
fluent in fire, not just the whispers, lisps, not just the *still there*
of powdered wigs, dry winds. Who wants a speckled
drape that folds as easy over smirch as fallen soldier?
This is rhetorical. Like, "What to the Negro
is the fourth of July?" A flag should be stitched with a fuse.

Jefferson said for each generation a flag. Maybe
he said Constitution. I once raised a high-top flag
of my hair, a fist, a leather medallion of the motherland.
I studied heraldry and maniples (which are not
what you might guess), little sails and banners
down to the vane of a feather. Because his kids were
rebel cities my father loved like Sherman. Because
I wanted history I could touch like the flank of a beast.

My wife's people are from San Salvador. They sent us
with a guard, his AK shouldered like a mandolin, among
anil-tinted shawls and jerseys, across tiled and pocked
concrete, and the gated stalls of El Centro. I felt sacred
as a goat there, too, as I did below the Mason-Dixon
where our only protection was the Fourteenth Amendment.

Afraid our Yankee plates would be read aggressive as a Jolly
Roger we rented a compact in Atlanta. Charleston, Savannah,
Montgomery, and after Birmingham we were broke.
Skipped Selma. Slept at B&Bs where my dreams power-
washed layers of footnotes and Februaries, revealing
the surreal sheen of Apollo Creed's trunks, the apocalyptic
Americana of Jacko moonwalking around a tinfoil Buzz
Aldrin planting the corporate ensign. Years passed. I grew

youthless in my dad-pants, but still puffed at pinwheels
and windsocks, launched glyphs of grillsmoke and one day
it came to me, as if commissioned, Theaster Gates's *Flag*
from old fire hoses, a couple dozen, like vertical blinds, no,
like cabin floorboards of canvas colored rusty, brick dust, some
cheerless drab-and-custard, beside a medley of vespertine
blues, hoses evoking landscapes of sackcloth and gunny,
texture of violence and tongues inflamed by shine, holy ghost.

Ross, Duchamp, Johns, et al., are integrated here with officers
of the peace, their dogs, and, in evidence, their pretend
tumescence Gates has hung to cure like pelts
or strips of jerky.

How did it feel to shield spirit with flesh? I mean,
what did it do to the body, water furry as the arm
of an arctic bear? What thirst did it ignite?

Gates's salute is a torch song, a rhythm
of hues marching over a pentimento of rhyme.
I approve its message, its pledge to birth a nation
of belonging and to teach that nation of the fire
shut up in our bones.

64

Pool Table

It belongs to the guy who used to cut
our lawn and has become by now my math tutor,
my sitter, my ersatz uncle—I call him *Chief.*
A sometime grad student and sometime sub
at Levitt Junior High. He seems to be polishing it, flaring
the angles of his stroke. He webs the table with his
mind's dotted lines. Beneath the Old Milwaukee
Tiffany lamp it smells of Thai stick and talcum.
Its felt as green as fresco hills spins English clean off the cue.
He strings together combinations hinged and whimsical
like flinty syllables playing with emphasis and breath
as he lectures me on the errorless vectors, velocity.
The spheres vanish like field mice as he runs the table
then lances one of the smoke rings shimmying like jellyfish
toward the dropped ceiling's popcorn panels
in his father's basement. He hikes himself up on
the rail, and sparks the dimming ember of his spliff
while I corral a spectrum in the field
of my embrace, arrange a bouquet of solids, stripes, each
numbered iris for Chief again to scatter the fragments
before my eyes like asteroids in an arcade game.
He claps a cloud of powder while he calls the four cross-
side, and then he calls me *Grasshopper,* tells me soon
I'm going to grasp all this like a pebble from his hand.

All God's Chillun

Late Sabbath morning and the laboring children
of modest, leafy districts will let stall their mowers
& whackers and set their trowels upon paving
stones, float flags of bandanas across beaded
brows and turn their chins toward the uprushing
draft to kite their breath-taking
bodies like milk pod seeds. While air brakes of semis
on the off-ramps anthem the children's lifting
like power chords from some distant rock opera,
the children will gyre off the lawns of Jersey silhouettes
thinning in the terrific noonday sun forming a jet
stream across wetlands & the flame-
scalloped Narrows. The children's outsized
shirts & pant waists we warn will not balloon
their longing for shores behind the horizon
or past the ozone patched with diminishing
shadows of the last battalion channeled into deserted
air shadows still crimpling like *crepe
de Chine* against the industrial haze. We panic,
can't fit all their images onto post office walls. And whose
flight are we talking here, anyway? Icarus or agony
of the American slave? They refuse to suggest
the angle of our sympathies. Young America! they
cry while we shake our heads picturing their bodies
dropping like spoons & watches we
admonish them their youth their bones their
fall into oceans where they'll glint and form
a railway only the ancients will read perched
on the detritus of commercial satellites,
and on car hoods, and athletic gear, all the gods
fettered to the machinery of our routine lives.

Wishing Well

Outside the Met a man walks up sun
tweaking the brim sticker on his Starter cap
and he says pardon me *Old School*, he
says you know is this a wishing well?
Yeah *Son* I say sideways over my shrug.
            Throw your bread on the water.
I tighten my chest wheezy as Rockaway beach
sand with a pull of faux smoke from my e-cig
to cozy the truculence I hotbox alone
and I am at the museum because it is not a bar.
Because he appears not to have changed
them in days I eye the heel-chewed hems
of his pants and think probably he will
ask me for fifty cents any minute now wait
for it. A smoke or something. Central Park displays
the frisking transparency of autumn. Tracing
paper sky, leaves like eraser crumbs gum
the pavement. As if deciphering celestial
script I squint and purse off toward the roof
line of the museum aloof as he fists two
pennies from his pockets mumbling and then
aloud my man he says hey my man I'm going
to make a wish for you too.
            I am laughing now so what you want
me to sign a waiver? He laughs along ain't
say all that he says but you do have to
hold my hand.   And close your eyes.

I make a starless night of my face before
he asks are you ready. Yeah *dawg* I'm ready.
Sure? Sure let's do this his rough hand

in mine inflates like a blood pressure cuff and I
squeeze back as if we are about to step together
from the sill of all resentment and timeless
toward the dreamsource of un-needing the two
of us hurtle sharing the cosmic breast
of plenitude when I hear the coins blink against
the surface and I cough up daylight like I've just
been dragged ashore. See now
you'll never walk alone he jokes and is about
to hand me back to the day he found me in
like I was a rubber duck and he says you got to let
go but I feel bottomless and I know he means
well though I don't believe
          and I feel myself shaking
my head no when he means let go his hand.

The Clinamen Improvisations

Deleuze & Guattari: *Making love is not just becoming as one, or even two, but becoming as a hundred thousand.*

Raise your eyes along the spires of Green-Wood Cemetery
or stand on the ball fields of Brooklyn College in Hopperesque
light. Quaker Parrots will appear to you like the visions
of St. Francis, lift the snatches of sound woven to make their
voices and call to you from their nests, a nation of cheer
trumpets and conch shells, a frenzied population of twitching,
toes. They seduce us not simply with their tropical verve. Listen
into the feathered shrubbery of their heat: they're chattering
lines from Emma Lazarus; they're trading fours on "Salt Peanuts";
they're mourning their cousin, the Carolina Parrot, reduced to
a flourish on ladies' headgear. Who flushed them from their ancestral
skies of Argentina? What love sustained the awareness of their bodies—
whether as chattel or deportees—such distance, and who speaks
for this Diaspora heedless of empire's mundane cartography?
If we ask why Brooklyn, we hear only our own reply:
If not here, where? then tease a final query from our minds like
thread from a lawn chair, parroting Hillel: *And if not now, when?*

Cervantes: *If it answers no other purpose, this long catalogue of authors will serve to give a surprising look of authority to your book.*

Vievee, Aaron, Camille, Ruth-E, Skoog, Timothy, Holly, Matejka, Tyehimba, Q, Major, Sandra, TSE, Che, Jennifer, Ravi, Joseph, Willie, Tracy, Tina, Ilya, Patricia, Jonathan, Cathy, Sue, Melissa, Rigoberto, Ada, Jen, Eisa, Kazim, Natasha, Singer, Kyle, Nester, Terrance, James, Sean, Elizabeth, Michael & Matthew, Erica D., Cate, Lyrae, Beckman, Jason, Jake (R.I.P.), Brenda, Amaud, Pavlic, Rosal, Marion, Joel, Susan, Nicky, Evie, Roger, Kevin, Sebastian, Latasha, Xochi, Oliver, Stacey Lynn, Shafer, Sarah, Shenoda, Paula, Patrick, Aracelis, Ben, Mark, Nick, Craig (R.I.P.), Murillo, Priscilla, Gabrielle, G.C., Jericho, Monica, Christian, Keene, Doug, Shane, Matthea, Prageeta, Van, Robin, Miguel, Dwayne, Ronaldo, Graber, Deborah, Uche, Alan, Mark, Tess, Matt, Kiaran, Frank X., Sherwin, Ross, Adam, Bino, Caitlin, Fred, Carl, Jenny, Randall, Tonya, Sharan, Cynthia, Aimee, Paula, Paul, Dawn, Mytili, Zapruder, Alex, Stuart, Katy, Anselm, Sedarat, Rich, Dante, Mark, Rebecca, Crystal, Erica W., Eduardo, Khalil, Jill, Myronn, Lillian, Marty, Cecily, Tara, Mendi, Jamaal

Alfred North Whitehead: *I have suffered a great deal from writers who have quoted this or that sentence of mine.*

Quotation marks tweeze text and lift it to gild the voice
of the speaker. Anonymous quotes bestow mystique like
a Venetian carnival mask that obscures in order to license.
(*Carne Vale*: farewell to flesh.) Chancing on a fetish for the
basis of taste, cannibals dined by firelight on the tongue
of the sacrifice. You? Incarnate the page, give words the body
you consume. Sound it out: *uroboros* whose mouth is a grave.
Your mouth merely gargles its ghost. Air quotes understate
cat claws to signify a type of predation. Read here about
the kids who "followed" J and M eight blocks home, fingers
flensing air like *Thriller* zombies. How fresh, how quotable,
the two men must have looked, hand in hand through
the hood. Let's say the kids wanted a snippet, a sound bite
to prize as the new exotic, a juju to brandish at mystery.
Say the beer bottle they threw conveyed a message: "You
have flavor." We suffer from an ancient envy. Hegel says,
"before setting out for a quotation, first dig two graves."

Epicurus: *The honor paid to a wise man is itself a great good for those who honor him.*

Sam Cooke reminds you how *Ol' Man River just keeps rolling*
and you begin to wonder what makes a river tick so you go sit
on Union Street Bridge to study the unruffled Gowanus Canal
with its tempting reflections and perfect your knack for reading
water's Om through the clockwork of the air and you think it's like
you which is not much of a river but wise enough water to hush your
regrets for the bloated casualties of your myriad indiscretions since
the first African was made to scoop the marsh to irrigate Dutch farms
until this moment when you see you are that African and you are
the Gowanus just as you are the baby whale lost and barging so far
along the canal you are blessed now and breaking and love this
one the *Daily News* will name Sludgy whom you will birth still
upon your bay at Red Hook after the sewer spills a glum baptismal
across his fontanel and children will stand around and amen
the Coast Guard atop the fly-flecked carcass preaching that wisdom
bends light into the eye of the whale where if you look close children
you'll find the water bears a flower and the flower bears your name

Kierkegaard: *He who does the work gives birth to his own father.*

Cooperate, say the doctors, and no one gets hurt. One day
they're roughing you up in an examination room. Next day
you imagine seeing them everywhere, tailing you, talking into
cufflinks in the Botanical Garden, spying over newspapers while
you play with your kids. Soon you're replaying your pop's chagrin
at how poorly you sport your own body, but this time you hear
Toss me the kidney, as if it were the football, that thing of no use
to you. The body is under duress. You drop warnings like bread
crumbs as your children tumble rough in the ash heaps of cherry
blossoms filed along the esplanade while the Parks Dept. drains
the near ravine. A hose rises from the leaf-rot like the shunt
that spigots your father's blood all week. Since he began to smell
of fatigue and carbolic soap, his locker room-style wolf
tickets nettle you everywhere. Evaporation will not relieve you
of the mirage you see approaching now, walking on clouds of sky-
blue shoe booties from the hospital. He is reaching out his hand.
He is offering the last chance he may give you to be worth a damn.

Notes

The italicized lines in "Copyright" are quoted from the Chicago *Tribune*, June 5, 1938.

"*ZoSo*" is the popular name for the symbol guitarist Jimmy Page chose to represent himself on the album, *Led Zeppelin IV*.

"Stay moment, thou art so fair," which appears in "Alienation Effects," is from Goethe's *Faust*.

Acknowledgments

Poems in this collection have appeared in the following journals and websites:

The American Poetry Review, The Awl, Beltway Poetry Quarterly, Black Renaissance/ Renaissance Noir, Boston Review, Callaloo, The Collagist, Harvard Review, JERRY, Meridian, Muzzle, The Nation, Painted Bride Quarterly, Ploughshares, Poet Lore, poetryfoundation.org, *P.S. 1/ MoMA* Newsletter, and *Tin House;* and in the anthologies, *Angles of Ascent: The Norton Anthology of Contemporary African American Poetry* (Norton, 2012), *A Face to Meet the Faces* (Univ. of Akron, 2012), *Best American Poetry* (Scribner, 2010), *Best American Poetry* (Scribner, 2014), and *So Much Things to Say* (Akashic, 2010).

Thanks

Vievee Francis, Ed Skoog, Jane Shore, David McAleavey, Marion Wrenn, Major Jackson, Thomas Sayers Ellis, Cornelius Eady, Tyehimba Jess, Charles Rowell, Rachel Eliza Griffiths, Amy Gerstler, Terrance Hayes, Robert Reid-Pharr, Ammiel Alcalay, and Wayne Koestenbaum; the communities of the CUNY Graduate Center, the *Callaloo* Creative Writing Workshop, Calabash International Writer's Foundation, The Frost Place, and the MacDowell Colony. And as always, the Moxie family.

Gregory Pardlo's first book, *Totem*, received the *American Poetry Review* / Honickman Prize in 2007. His poems have appeared in *American Poetry Review*, *Boston Review*, *The Nation*, *Ploughshares*, *Tin House*, as well as anthologies including *Angles of Ascent*: the Norton Anthology of Contemporary African American Poetry and two editions of *Best American Poetry*. He is the recipient of a New York Foundation for the Arts Fellowship and a fellowship for translation from the National Endowment for the Arts. He has received other fellowships from the *New York Times*, the MacDowell Colony, the Lotos Club Foundation, and Cave Canem. An associate editor of *Callaloo*, he is currently a teaching fellow in Undergraduate Writing at Columbia University.